The Ohio Bucket List

100 Ways to Have a Real Ohio Experience

Michael Crisp

REMIX BOOKS

Published in Georgetown, KY

United States of America

Remix Books
PO Box 1303
Georgetown, KY 40324

www.ohiobucketlist.com

Cover Design by
Logan Singleton

Layout by
Kevin Kifer
www.k2-technology.com

ISBN 978-1-6284-7545-6

First Edition

legal disclaimer

This book is designed to provide information, entertainment, and motivation to our readers. It is sold with the understanding that the publisher is not engaged to render any type of physical, psychological, legal, or any other advice.

Participation in the activities listed may be dangerous, illegal, and could lead to arrest, serious injury, or death.

The content in this book is the sole expression and opinion of its author and not necessarily that of the publisher. No warranties or guarantees are expressed or implied.

Neither the publisher nor the author shall be liable for any physical, psychological, emotional, financial, or commercial damages, including, but not limited to, special, incidental, consequential, or other damages.

Our views and rights are the same: you are responsible for your own choices, actions, and results.

Orville and Wilbur Wright, pioneers of aviation.
Photo courtesy the Library of Congress

dedication

For Andrew, Rhiannon, Scott and Sandy.
Great friends make for great adventures!

bucket list:

a number of experiences or achievements that a person hopes to have or accomplish during their lifetime.

Courtesy of the Oxford American Dictionary

Most Ohioans would agree that there's simply no place quite like Ohio. As a child, I have fond memories of going to Riverfront Stadium to watch the Big Red Machine, seeing Ken Anderson quarterback the Bengals to (occasional) victory, and marveling at the Eiffel Tower replica at King's Island. As I grew up and started my own family, I was able to venture farther into the state and experience much more of Ohio.

In writing this book, I wanted to combine all of the quintessential "things to do" in Ohio with some of the more obscure experiences that the state has to offer. Sure, almost everyone has heard about the Rock and Roll Hall of Fame in Cleveland, but how many people know that Dean Martin was born in Steubenville and that the city hosts an annual festival each June in his honor? With that being said, I knew that a "bucket list" book was needed in order to help inspire a series of adventures for everyone who loves the buckeye state and the vast array of experiences that it has to offer.

While writing this book, I came across a handful of items that helped me with my research. There were several websites devoted to traveling in Ohio, most notably *DiscoverOhio.com*, which offered a handful of wonderful suggestions that I added to the list.

One of the biggest inspirations for this book is my good friend, David Sloan. David is an author (and all-around renaissance man) who resides in Key West, Florida. David wrote *The Key West Bucket List*, which met with great success. Last year he convinced me (rather easily) to write *The Kentucky Bucket List*, a book that allowed me to combine two of my passions, writing and travel.

Whether you are from Ohio, live here now, or are planning a visit, I hope that you enjoy this book and the experiences that are within it.

what to expect

1. No Instruction Manual:

This book isn't an instructional guidebook that tells you what to do and how to do it. The object here is for you to seek out each of the items in this book and then enjoy these experiences on your own.

2. Adventure and Challenge:

Some of the items on this list are easy to accomplish, some are more difficult, and others are downright close to impossible. Don't worry - no one is watching you or grading your performance. Take each adventure one by one, at your own pace, and you will get the most out of this book.

3. Inspiration:

I've often been accused of being a "know-it-all" (especially after I've had a few cold beverages), but I'm definitely not a fountain of wisdom. That's why I called in the experts. Mark Twain, Helen Keller, Ralph Waldo Emerson, and Thomas Edison are all contributors with quotes that lend a deeper meaning to each adventure.

4. Satisfaction:

Whether you fill out the list at the end of this book with a fat red pen, or you take each of these journeys in your mind from the comfort of your favorite chair, this book should leave you with a profound sense of satisfaction. You will have so much fun with this book that you'll probably feel like sharing your own thoughts and stories with others. Feel free to visit our Facebook page to share your musings, experiences, photos, and new additions to the list.

Enjoy,
Michael Crisp

"Nothing is a waste of time if you use the experience wisely."

- Auguste Rodin

1

See a Reds Game
Great American Ballpark,
Cincinnati

*"Slumps are like a soft bed. They're easy to get
into and hard to get out of."*

- Johnny Bench

2

Sleep in a Castle
Landoll's Mohican Castle, Loudonville

"A man's home may seem to be his castle on the outside; inside is more often his nursery."

- Clare Booth Luce

3

Spend a Day at the Beach

Maumee Bay State Park, Oregon

"One cannot collect all the beautiful shells on the beach. One can collect only a few, and they are more beautiful if they are few."

- Anne Morrow Lindbergh

4

Explore an Amish Community

Millersburg, Holmesville, Walnut Creek or Berlin

"Simplicity is the ultimate sophistication."

- Leonardo da Vinci

5

Find Your Dream Car
Snook's Dream Cars Museum, Bowling Green

"Never lend your car to anyone to whom you have given birth."

- Erma Bombeck

6

Go Stargazing

Planetarium at Boonshoft Museum of Discovery, Dayton

"For the wise man looks into space and he knows there is no limited dimensions."

- Lao Tzu

7

Visit the Rock and Roll Hall of Fame
Cleveland

"Rock and roll is music for the neck downwards."

- Keith Richards

8

Spot a Bald Eagle
Crane Creek State Park, Jerusalem

"You cannot fly like an eagle with the wings of a wren."

- William Henry Hudson

9

Shop at an Outlet Mall
Jeffersonville, Lodi or Aurora

"The quickest way to know a woman is to go shopping with her"

- Marcelene Cox

10

Play a Game of Cornhole

Anywhere, But Preferably While Tailgating

"Games lubricate the body and the mind."

- Benjamin Franklin

11

Be Inspired
Cincinnati Art Museum, Cincinnati

"You can't wait for inspiration. You have to go after it with a club."

- Jack London

12

See the Floodwall Murals
Portsmouth

"The walls we build around us to keep sadness out also keeps out the joy."

- Jim Rohn

13

Hike a Trail
Hocking Hills State Park, Logan

"It's the way you ride the trail that counts."

- Dale Evans

14

Take Your Kids to the Great Lakes Science Center

Great Lakes Science Center, Cleveland

"Research is what I'm doing when I don't know what I'm doing."

- Wernher von Braun

15

See an Ohio State Football Game
Ohio Stadium, Columbus

"Football is, after all, a wonderful way to get rid of your aggressions without going to jail for it."

- Woody Hayes

Photo courtesy of the Allen County Museum, Lima, Ohio

16

See the Shay Locomotive

Allen County Museum, Lima

"I never travel without my diary. One should always have something sensational to read in the train."

- Oscar Wilde

17

Take a Picture of the Marblehead Lighthouse
Lakeside Marblehead

"Man cannot discover new oceans unless he has the courage to lose sight of the shore."

- Andre Gide

18

Venture to the Top of the Eiffel Tower

King's Island, Mason

"A lot of people are afraid of heights. Not me, I'm afraid of widths."

- Steven Wright

19

Explore a Cave
Seneca Caverns, Bellevue

"It is better to light a candle than curse the darkness."

- Eleanor Roosevelt

20

Admire an Architectural Wonder

Frank Lloyd Wright House, Oberlin

"Creativity is allowing yourself to make mistakes. Art is knowing which ones to keep."

- Scott Adams

Photo courtesy of Kevin Kifer

21

Have a Cold One
At a Local Microbrewery

"Milk is for babies. When you grow up you have to drink beer."

- Arnold Schwarzenegger

22

Take a Ride on the Goodyear Blimp
Akron

"There is one spectacle grander than the sea, that is the sky; there is one spectacle grander than the sky, that is the interior of the soul."

- Victor Hugo

23

See a Manatee
Columbus Zoo, Columbus

"The sea, once it casts its spell, holds one in its net of wonder forever."

- Jacques Cousteau

24

Walk Through the Interurban Tunnel
Blackhand Gorge State Nature Preserve, Heath

"Walking with a friend in the dark is better than walking alone in the light."

- Helen Keller

The Interurban Tunnel at Blackhand Gorge State Nature
Preserve, Heath, Ohio.
Photo courtesy of the Library of Congress

25

Hold a Handful of Buckeye Seeds
Anywhere

"With every deed you are sowing a seed, though the harvest you may not see."

- Ella Wheeler Wilcox

26

See a Waterfall

Chagrin Falls

"In all things of nature there is something marvelous."

- Aristotle

27

Visit the Cincinnati Museum Center

Cincinnati Museum Center at Union Terminal, Cincinnati

"A people without the knowledge of their past history, origin and culture is like a tree without roots."

- Marcus Garvey

28

Ride a Trolley
Put-in-Bay

"Hope is like the sun, which, as we journey toward it, casts the shadow of our burden behind us."

- Samuel Smiles

29

See a Moon Rock

Armstrong Air & Space Museum,
Wapakoneta

"I believe that every human has a finite number of heartbeats. I don't intend to waste any of mine."

- Neil Armstrong

30

Listen to Bluegrass Music
Southern Ohio Opry, Lucasville

"Music washes away from the soul the dust of everyday life."

- Berthold Auerbach

31

Feed a Giraffe
African Safari Wildlife Park, Port Clinton

"Until one has loved an animal a part of one's soul remains unawakened."

- Anatole France

32

See the World's Largest Basket

Longaberger Homestead & Basket Factory, Frazeysburg

"The wise man puts all his eggs in one basket and watches the basket."

- Andrew Carnegie

33

See a Bengals Game
Paul Brown Stadium, Cincinnati

"When you win, say nothing. When you lose, say less."

- Paul Brown

34

Pay Your Respects to a U.S. President

McKinley Monument, Canton

"Seek not greatness, but seek truth and you will find both."

- Horace Mann

35

Go Ice Skating
Lock 3, Akron

"The problem with winter sports is that - follow me closely here - they generally take place in the winter."

- Dave Barry

36

Visit the National Road/ Zane Grey Museum
New Conchord

"Love of man for woman, love of woman for man. That's the nature, the meaning, the best of life itself."

- Zane Grey

37

Buy an Exotic Food

Jungle Jim's International Market, Fairfield

"One should eat to live, not live to eat."

- Moliere

38

Dance to Polka Music

Anywhere, But Preferably After a Few Beverages

"Polka is the happiest music this side of heaven."

- Frank Yankovic

39

See a Play
Play House Center, Cleveland

"The pit of a theatre is the one place where the tears of virtuous and wicked men alike are mingled."

- Denis Diderot

The Taft Museum of Art, Cincinnati, Ohio.
Photo courtesy of the Library of Congress

40

Behold a Masterpiece
Taft Museum of Art, Cincinnati

*"Art enables us to find ourselves and lose
ourselves at the same time."*

- Thomas Merton

41

Race Your Car

Mid Ohio Sports Car Course, Lexington

"Fix your eyes on perfection and you make almost everything speed towards it."

- William Ellery Channing

42

Attend the Ohio State Fair

Ohio Expo Center, Columbus

"All the events of your life are there because you have drawn them there. What you choose to do with them is up to you."

- Richard Bach

43

Behold the Statue of Jesus
Solid Rock Church, Monroe

"Christianity helps us face the music even when we don't like the tune."

- Phillips Brooks

44

Ride a Bicycle
Xenia Station, Xenia

"Life is like a ten speed bicycle. Most of us have gears we never use."

- Charles M. Schulz

45

See a Cavaliers Game
Quicken Loans Arena, Cleveland

"Basketball doesn't build character. It reveals it."

- Author Unknown

46

Let Freedom Ring

National Underground Railroad Freedom Center, Cincinnati

"Is freedom anything else than the right to live as we wish? Nothing else."

- Epictetus

47

Go Camping
Indian Lake State Park, Indian Lake

"Slumber not in the tents of your fathers. The world is advancing."

- Giuseppe Mazzini

48

Win Big at a Casino
Horseshoe Casino, Cleveland and Cincinnati

"I like to play blackjack. I'm not addicted to gambling, I'm addicted to sitting in a semi-circle."

- Mitch Hedberg

49

Attend the Dean Martin Festival
Steubenville

"I feel sorry for people who don't drink. They wake up in the morning and that's the best they're going to feel all day."

- Dean Martin

50

Explore a Submarine
USS Cod, Cleveland

"Life is like the ocean, it goes up and down."

- Vanessa Paradis

51

Go Shopping at Kroger™
Anywhere, But Preferably With a Kroger™
Card

"Recreational shopping is the shortest distance between two points: you and broke."

- Victoria Moran

52

See a Hemlock Tree
Wakheena Nature Preserve, Sugar Grove

"Solitary trees, if they grow at all, grow strong."

- Winston Churchill

53

Attend a Dinner Party
Buckingham Meeting House, Newark

"At a dinner party one should eat wisely but not too well, and talk well but not too wisely."

- W. Somerset Maugham

54

Visit the Pro Football Hall of Fame
Canton

"Glory lies in the attempt to reach one's goal and not in reaching it."

- Mahatma Gandhi

55

Walk the Halls of the Ohio Statehouse

Ohio Statehouse, Columbus

"The best minds are not in government. If any were, business would steal them away."

- Ronald Reagan

56

Take a Riverboat Cruise on the Ohio River

Anywhere in Southern Ohio

"You cannot step into the same river twice."

- Heraclitus

57

Admire a Masterpiece
Cleveland Museum of Art, Cleveland

"A picture is a poem without words."

- Horace

58

Explore Serpent Mound
Peebles

"If a man is as wise as a serpent, he can afford to be as harmless as a dove."

- Cheyenne Proverb

59

Hear a Concert at Music Hall

Cincinnati

"One good thing about music, when it hits you, you feel no pain."

- Bob Marley

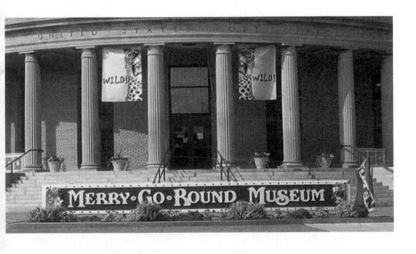

The Merry-Go-Round Museum, Sandusky, Ohio
Photo courtesy of The Merry-Go-Round Museum

60

Ride a Carousel
Merry-Go-Round Museum, Sandusky

"There is always one moment in childhood when the door opens and lets the future in."

- Graham Greene

61

See an Opera
The Ohio Light Opera, Wooster

"No good opera plot can be sensible, for people do not sing when they are feeling sensible."

- W.H. Auden

62

Enjoy Barbeque Ribs at the Montgomery Inn
Cincinnati

"An empty belly is the best cook."

- Estonian Proverb

63

Play a Round of Golf at Muirfield Village
Dublin

"I like trying to win. That's what golf is all about."

- Jack Nicklaus

64

See a Shark

Greater Cleveland Aquarium, Cleveland

"As they say about sharks, it's not the ones you see that you have to worry about, it's the ones you don't see."

- David Blaine

65

Celebrate History

Perry's Victory and International Peace
Memorial, Put-in-Bay

*"We are made wise not by the recollection of our
past, but by the responsibility of our future."*

- George Bernard Shaw

66

Stand Inside Air Force One

National Museum of the United States Air Force, Dayton

"To achieve, you need thought. You have to know what you are doing and that's real power."

- Ayn Rand

67

Buy Something Unique
West Side Market, Cleveland

"You are unique, and if that is not fulfilled, then something has been lost."

- Martha Graham

68

See the Butterfly Show
Krohn Conservatory, Eden Park

"Never lose an opportunity of seeing anything beautiful, for beauty is God's handwriting."

- Ralph Waldo Emerson

69

Gaze at the Glacial Grooves

North Side of Kelley's Island, Port Clinton

"Travel is more than the seeing of sights; it is a change that goes on, deep and permanent, in the ideas of the living."

- Miriam Beard

70

Watch a Sunset from the Top of the Carew Tower

Carew Tower & Observation Deck, Cincinnati

"It is almost impossible to watch a sunset and not dream."

- Bern Williams

71

Ride a Roller Coaster at Cedar Point
Sandusky

"Accept the challenges so that you can feel the exhilaration of victory."

- George S. Patton

72

Stroll Through a Garden
Stan Hywet Hall and Gardens, Akron

"A garden is a grand teacher. It teaches patience and careful watchfulness; it teaches industry and thrift; above all it teaches entire trust."

- Gertrude Jekyll

73

Honor Our Soldiers
Ohio Veterans Memorial Park, Clinton

"Great achievement is usually born of great sacrifice, and is never the result of selfishness."

- Napoleon Hill

74

See an Indians Game
Progressive Field, Cleveland

"Life comes down to honesty and doing what's right. That's what's most important."

- Bob Feller

75

Perform an Experiment
Center of Science and Industry, Columbus

"Opportunity is missed by most people because it is dressed in overalls and looks like work."

- Thomas Edison

76

Walk Across the Purple People Bridge
Cincinnati

"We build too many walls and not enough bridges."

- Isaac Newton

77

Search for a Ghost
Mansfield Reformatory, Mansfield

"True love is like ghosts, which everyone talks about and few have seen."

**- Francois de La
Rochefoucauld**

78

Visit the Paul Laurence Dunbar House
Dayton

"We wear the mask that grins and lies, it hides our cheeks and shades our eyes."

- Paul Laurence Dunbar

Dinosaur exhibit at the Cleveland
Museum of Natural History, Cleveland, Ohio
Photo courtesy of the Library of Congress

79

See a Dinosaur

Cleveland Museum of Natural History,
Cleveland

"I think we like to be put in our place by awesome things. Dinosaurs do that."

- Sue Hendrickson

80

Pick Raspberries
Robert Rothschild Farms, Urbana

"Patience is bitter, but its fruit is sweet."

- Jean-Jacques Rousseau

81

Become Part of a Painting
Topiary Park, Columbus

"Good painting is the kind that looks like sculpture."

- Michelangelo

82

See an Exotic Animal
Cincinnati Zoo, Cincinnati

"A zoo is an excellent place to study the habits of human beings."

- Evan Esar

83

Use Your Imagination
Toledo Imagination Station, Toledo

"You can't use up creativity. The more you use, the more you have."

- Maya Angelou

84

Sing "Hang On Sloopy"
Anywhere, But Preferably at a Pub with Good Friends

"The only thing better than singing is more singing."

- Ella Fitzgerald

85

Get Your Wings

Dayton Aviation Heritage National Historic Park

"To invent an airplane is nothing. To build one is something. But to fly is everything."

- Otto Lilienthal

86

Go Fishing for Walleye
Lake Erie

"There's a fine line between fishing and just standing on the shore like an idiot."

- Steven Wright

87

Watch a Joust
Ohio Renaissance Festival, Harveysburg

"If human beings had genuine courage, they'd wear their costumes every day of the year, not just on Halloween."

- Doug Coupland

88

See a Browns Game from the Dawg Pound
FirstEnergy Stadium, Cleveland

"The game of life is a lot like football. You have to tackle your problems, block your fears, and score your points when you get the opportunity."

- Lewis Grizzard

89

Take a Winery Tour

Anytime, But Preferably in the Summer

"Wine is bottled poetry."

- Robert Louis Stevenson

90

Eat a Bratwurst
Bucyrus

"Older people shouldn't eat health food; they need all the preservatives they can get."

- Robert Orben

91

See a Monet
Dayton Art Institute, Dayton

"Everyone discusses my art and pretends to understand, as if it were necessary to understand, when it is simply necessary to love."

- Claude Monet

92

Devour a Cincinnati-Style Chili Dog

Gold Star Chili or Skyline Chili

"My children refuse to eat anything that hasn't danced around on television."

- Erma Bombeck

93

Walk the Deck of the Santa Maria

Santa Maria Replica Ship, Columbus

"There is no better high than discovery."

- E.O. Wilson

94

Visit the House From "A Christmas Story"
"A Christmas Story" House, Cleveland

"The main reason Santa is so jolly is because he knows where all the bad girls live."

- George Carlin

95

Drive Through the Mull Covered Bridge
Fremont

"To live permanently away from the country is a form of slow death."

- Esther Meynell

96

Visit a Mill

Lanterman's Mill, Youngstown

"Life is a grindstone, and whether it grinds a man down or polishes him up depends on the stuff he's made of."

- Josh Billings

97

Toss a Coin in the Tylor Davidson Fountain
Fountain Square, Cincinnati

"Time is the coin of your life. It is the only coin you have, and only you can determine how it will be spent. Be careful lest you let other people spend it for you."

- Carl Sandburg

98

Ride a Train

Cuyahoga Valley National Park, Brecksville

"The only way to be sure of catching a train is to miss the one before it."

- Gilbert K. Chesterton

99

See the Orchids at The Franklin Park Conservatory

The Franklin Park Conservatory, Columbus

"Earth laughs in flowers."

- Ralph Waldo Emerson

100

Have Ice Cream With the Author of This Book
Graeter's Ice Cream, Cincinnati

"Ice cream is happiness condensed."

- Jessie Lane Adams

i did it

Check off your accomplishments with the writing utensil of your choice:

- [ ] 1. See a Reds Game
- [ ] 2. Sleep in a Castle
- [ ] 3. Spend a Day at the Beach
- [ ] 4. Explore an Amish Community
- [ ] 5. Find Your Dream Car
- [ ] 6. Go Stargazing
- [ ] 7. Visit the Rock and Roll Hall of Fame
- [ ] 8. Spot a Bald Eagle
- [ ] 9. Shop at an Outlet Mall
- [ ] 10. Play a Game of Cornhole
- [ ] 11. Be Inspired
- [ ] 12. See the Floodwall Murals
- [ ] 13. Hike a Trail
- [ ] 14. Take Your Kids to the Great Lakes Science Center
- [ ] 15. See an Ohio State Football Game
- [ ] 16. See the Shay Locomotive
- [ ] 17. Take a Picture of the Marblehead Lighthouse
- [ ] 18. Venture to the Top of the Eiffel Tower
- [ ] 19. Explore a Cave
- [ ] 20. Admire an Architectural Wonder
- [ ] 21. Have a Cold One
- [ ] 22. Take a Ride on the Goodyear Blimp

- ☐ 23. See a Manatee
- ☐ 24. Walk Through the Interurban Tunnel
- ☐ 25. Hold a Handful of Buckeye Seeds
- ☐ 26. See a Waterfall
- ☐ 27. Visit the Cincinnati Museum Center
- ☐ 28. Ride a Trolley
- ☐ 29. See a Moon Rock
- ☐ 30. Listen to Bluegrass Music
- ☐ 31. Feed a Giraffe
- ☐ 32. See the World's Largest Basket
- ☐ 33. See a Bengals Game
- ☐ 34. Pay Your Respects to a U.S. President
- ☐ 35. Go Ice Skating
- ☐ 36. Visit the National Road/Zane Grey Museum
- ☐ 37. Buy an Exotic Food
- ☐ 38. Dance to Polka Music
- ☐ 39. See a Play
- ☐ 40. Behold a Masterpiece
- ☐ 41. Race Your Car
- ☐ 42. Attend the Ohio State Fair
- ☐ 43. Behold the Statue of Jesus
- ☐ 44. Ride a Bicycle
- ☐ 45. See a Cavaliers Game
- ☐ 46. Let Freedom Ring
- ☐ 47. Go Camping
- ☐ 48. Win Big at a Casino
- ☐ 49. Attend the Dean Martin Festival
- ☐ 50. Explore a Submarine
- ☐ 51. Go Shopping at Kroger™
- ☐ 52. See a Hemlock Tree

- ☐ 53. Attend a Dinner Party
- ☐ 54. Visit the Pro Football Hall of Fame
- ☐ 55. Walk the Halls of the Ohio Statehouse
- ☐ 56. Take a Riverboat Cruise on the Ohio River
- ☐ 57. Admire a Masterpiece
- ☐ 58. Explore Serpent Mound
- ☐ 59. Hear a Concert at Music Hall
- ☐ 60. Ride a Carousel
- ☐ 61. See an Opera
- ☐ 62. Enjoy Barbeque Ribs at the Montgomery Inn
- ☐ 63. Play a Round of Golf at Muirfield Village
- ☐ 64. See a Shark
- ☐ 65. Celebrate History
- ☐ 66. Stand Inside Air Force One
- ☐ 67. Buy Something Unique
- ☐ 68. See the Butterfly Show
- ☐ 69. Gaze at the Glacial Grooves
- ☐ 70. Watch a Sunset from the Top of the Carew Tower
- ☐ 71. Ride a Roller Coaster at Cedar Point
- ☐ 72. Stroll Through a Garden
- ☐ 73. Honor Our Soldiers
- ☐ 74. See an Indians Game
- ☐ 75. Perform an Experiment
- ☐ 76. Walk Across the Purple People Bridge
- ☐ 77. Search for a Ghost
- ☐ 78. Visit the Paul Laurence Dunbar House
- ☐ 79. See a Dinosaur
- ☐ 80. Pick Raspberries

- ☐ 81. Become Part of a Painting
- ☐ 82. See an Exotic Animal
- ☐ 83. Use Your Imagination
- ☐ 84. Sing "Hang On Sloopy"
- ☐ 85. Get Your Wings
- ☐ 86. Go Fishing for Walleye
- ☐ 87. Watch a Joust
- ☐ 88. See a Browns Game from the Dawg Pound
- ☐ 89. Take a Winery Tour
- ☐ 90. Eat a Bratwurst
- ☐ 91. See a Monet
- ☐ 92. Devour a Cincinnati-Style Chili Dog
- ☐ 93. Walk the Deck of the Santa Maria
- ☐ 94. Visit the House From "A Christmas Story"
- ☐ 95. Drive Through the Mull Covered Bridge
- ☐ 96. Visit a Mill
- ☐ 97. Toss a Coin in the Tylor Davidson Fountain
- ☐ 98. Ride a Train
- ☐ 99. See the Orchids at The Franklin Park Conservatory
- ☐ 100. Have Ice Cream With the Author of This Book

add to the list

- [ ] 101. _____
- [ ] 102. _____
- [ ] 103. _____
- [ ] 104. _____
- [ ] 105. _____
- [ ] 106. _____
- [ ] 107. _____
- [ ] 108. _____
- [ ] 109. _____
- [ ] 110. _____
- [ ] 111. _____
- [ ] 112. _____
- [ ] 113. _____
- [ ] 114. _____
- [ ] 115. _____
- [ ] 116. _____
- [ ] 117. _____
- [ ] 118. _____
- [ ] 119. _____
- [ ] 120. _____
- [ ] 121. _____
- [ ] 122. _____
- [ ] 123. _____
- [ ] 124. _____
- [ ] 125. _____

special thanks

Kevin Kifer
Scott Hall
Scott McBrayer
Andrew Moore
David Sloan
Kenny Rice
Han Fan
John McDaniel
Conner Crisp
Marge Crisp
Ryder McCraith
Pamela Holland
Karey Riddell
Logan Singleton
Dawn Brackman
Stacey Gillespie
Chuck Girmann
Angie Girmann

The Ohio Bucket List
written by
Michael Crisp

book jacket text and "what to expect" text written by
Michael Crisp and David Sloan

Other Books by Michael Crisp

The Kentucky Bucket List

The Tennessee Bucket List

Murder in the Mountains:
The Muriel Baldridge Story

The Making of The Very Worst Thing

Films Directed by Michael Crisp Include:

The Very Worst Thing

When Happy Met Froggie

Legendary: When Baseball
Came to the Bluegrass

A Cut Above: The Legend of Larry Roberts

Available at Local Bookstores
and Online at Amazon.com

"I love Ohio."

- Dave Chappelle